DAUGHTERS, HERE | DAUGHTERS, GONE

Poems

Scot Siegel

First U.S. edition 2018

Editor and Publisher: Laura LeHew

Proofreaders: Quinton Hallett
                        Nancy Carol Moody

Cover Art: The untitled photograph used for the cover is
                        copyrighted by James Manusos. All rights reserved.

Copyright © 2018   Scot Siegel

Uttered Chaos
PO Box 50638
Eugene, OR 97405
www.utteredchaos.org

ISBN: 978-0-9998334-0-7

for Lianne and Caroline

Table of Contents

"Daddy, life is a dream that is real. Look, there's construction out there!"

—Lianne, age 5

"Dad, did you know that our voices are not attached to our bodies?"

—Caroline, age 5

Three Moments of Silence

Here is the toddler learning to walk.
This is the day she packs for college.
Here is the way you give her away
as though she were yours to give.

Sunshine

Daddy, I like it when the sun
Interrupts us…

Oh, yes… Yes, like when it
Burns through fog, splashing leaves,
And touches the side of your face
Warm as your mother's kiss?

No, Dad, just the sun
All by itself—
       no kiss
       no flame
       no leaves—

Just the sun's sudden rays
Pouring down
Right here
Right now

On you and me.

Without Supervision

After a hard
City snow
Followed by a stiff
East wind
That shakes the house
Like a sifter
Loosing powder from sills
Scattering it
Everywhere –
The sky cracks open
Unfolds a hand
Hands over a yolk
The sun alights
On a bridge
City at a standstill
The sky gloats
Like a child
Who's baked
Linzer Torte
For the very
First time.

Keeper

Daddy, when I raise my hand like this
And brush the sky in front of us

I am really patting the horse I miss
The one I met once

On that family trip, when you
Took us to the mountains.

Sometimes, I dream we live there,
And the dream goes on –

Dad, cool mornings like this
When I lower my hand

I feel his mane like the wind
Through my fingers.

You and Mom and Sister
Are there

And his name is Keeper.

Patient and Helper
—after Lianne at Forward Stride Therapeutic Center

First day on the job
She stands ready
Listening:

Here's the red clicker
For catching Dancer.

If you don't know how
Ask a helper. Don't use it
On any other horse.

Ladybug's easy.
Keep an eye on Ruby
And don't leave

Tucker's hay soaking
Anywhere near
Blesi's stall.

If windy
Keep Ed inside…

Fluorescent lights crackle
A crucial memorial
For summer insects.

The boy who possesses
Part or all of an extra
Twenty-first chromosome

Steps toward the unnamed mare
Who shuffles and clops
In the darkened rear stall.

Down Syndrome children
Have impaired cognitive
And physical growth

Facial characteristics
Identifiable at pregnancy or birth.
Though some features appear

In persons lacking
The extra chromosome:
   Shorter limbs
   Poor muscle tone

   Simian crease in the palms
   And those almond-shaped eyes
   That can leave you guessing

   About the larger than
   Normal spaces between
   Big and second toes

   And those wide smiles.

In the faint barn light
My daughter moves like an angel.
Crisscrossing the aisle
She's a hummingbird,
Quick, then still.

Her hand guiding
The boy's hand
They brush Blesi down
And begin with
The hoof pick.

Quiet down there
Impossible now to tell
The difference
Between patient
And helper.

Witnessed on a Country Road

Once, a great brown cloud billowed
From the back of a tractor called Now.
Overtook power poles, horses,
Abandoned orchards, then the road.

Our truck slowed of its own accord,
Hugged the shoulder. The cloud
Crawled forth like a slave,
Cloistering us.

You wanted to know,
What is happening?
The digital compass of my
Parenting stalled: No synapses

No brilliant sparks clicked our
Gritty windows. Then moths.
Decapitated deer. Oncoming semis.
Airplanes. Earthquakes.

Unnamed wars. We took a stand,
Held hands like Jews fleeing Pharaoh.
Pressed our eyes to the window. Sang,
As the dust storm lifted.

Independence Day

On the long drive
To the beach
We have little to say.

On the way home
We solve most of
The world's problems.

We Fill Our Pockets
—after Caroline, age 9

I think of you under your sheets hiding
A storm of your own making
Building outside the window.
Dreams, like bats, tug our tents
Yours and mine, from afar.

We are geologists
We fill our pockets
With carnelian agates
And less beautiful
Specimens: clam shells

Split and riddled by
Sea lice. False fossils
Bits of iron slag hauled
In t-shirt rucksacks
From the shoreline.

We keep them close—
Talismans to ward off
Nightmares and stranger
Premonitions—
We care for them

Like brittle birds
The way I care for these words
Little glass origami
I carry down the mountain
To tell you some day.

Equinox

Summer and Fall
Slowly twirl –
Then switch hands

Trick-or-Treat
—for Lianne and Caroline

One of you is the girl-wizard.
The other, Tina Fey
Impersonating Sarah Palin.

Democrats on our street eat it up.
Republicans adore you.
One couple invites you inside.

We do not know their names
But it does not matter.
We pay too much for insurance

But are grateful for our health.
9/11 still stings, but we think
That war is coming to an end.

The Recession has not yet hit.
We want the black man to win.
A woman could be next.

This is what was like, raising you,
In 2008, when SNL was still quaint
And anything was possible.

Imagine that, if you can.

Trumpets

Is this sadness a new form of solace
Or chrysalis pre-revolution?

What does normalization mean
Under a post-truth regime?

Our country has a hole in its heart
The size of our country.

Though even a man filled with hate
Is prone to paper cuts and spider bites.

If his heart fails in the middle of the night
We will know by the absence of tweets

And flash mobs of birdsong.

Daughters, Here

I know America
Has let us down again,
And again, and again...

Don't worry,
We can count on
This country—

The country within
The country of the heart
Has no border—

And we are eternally
Optimistic
About the direction

You are taking us.

Time's Up, and Here You Are

You can tell the ones
Who've escaped

Having beat that which
Others thought was fate—

Lightness in her step,
A subdued giddiness

And ease with which
She navigates the news—

A fire in the eyes
That says, *You too*

Can carry yourself,
Just like this.

Dog

Our dog has two hearts:
One that keeps her warm.

The other jumpstarts my heart
When I forget to breathe.

Commencement

They say it means *beginning*
As though your life is a poem

That is not yet written.
Some lyric lies hidden

Deep in your heart—
A song somewhere apart

From this world—
And you long to hear it.

Valedictory

If you were not meant
To follow

Be unconventional
In a mild-mannered way.

Put yourself at risk, emotionally,
Intellectually, simultaneously.

Take a leadership role –
Say unpopular things

While nodding insistently
And lending a hand.

Parhelion (Sundog)
—for Lianne, after winter break

At twenty-one, you climb the Santiam sled hill
As you've done so many times before,
At least in my memory, which experiences
Everything you do as an endless echo.

The same gait at five, or how I remember five:
Determined, yet playful, each stride intentional.
Swing dancer, you look back every ten steps
Admiring your own footwork—amplitude,

Altitude—each step a bit faster. I wave, but
You do not look up. I wave again, and point,
But you do not see what I am saying. Behind you,
A sundog, an ice rainbow, skitters across

The bluest sky ever. I meant to tell you,
It was a perfect day.

Four Tenses

There is no present like the present.
It is the gift that keeps on giving.

The future offers everything, promises
Nothing, and delivers something else.

The past cannot remember what the future
Tried explaining to the present.

Truth occurs when Past, Present and Future
All sing in the same key.

An open mind

is a periscope over the light and dark swells of a heart.

History, The Homemaker

History is independently wealthy.
She has so many rooms, she's lost track.
History is hoarse from having to repeat herself.
She is losing her mind but has all the time in the world.
History knows how worlds come to an end.
She lived in a convent once but was caught revising the Scripture.
History is a wizard at math and believes in home remedies.
History is not the Virgin Mary, she kicks the baby out with the father.
History craves something savory for a late-night snack.
She hates the History Channel more than science fiction.
History critiques The Great British Baking Show reclining in a bath.
History barters the family jewels for bourbon.
She hawks the silver for food.
History prefers cardamom to cinnamon.
When History cooks, her moods swing like the moons of Jupiter.
History has a habit of leaving the oven on.
She's burned the house down so many times
You'd think she does it for the rush.
Only Courage and Hope can save her; they rebuild the house
With iron and cedar, and treat the linens with camphor.
History was arrested once for shooting up Fiction.
When drunk, she revises her autobiography to cheer herself up.
Everyone tells History his or her secrets.
History is the headmistress at the school of hard knocks.
She does not wear pumps or grow her hair out for you.
History loves Allegory and wears Paradox to the ball.
She leaves early, something boiling at home.
History cooks for armies.
She fills your plate with more than you can eat.
History knows the homeless are royalty.
She keeps the leftovers warm for centuries.
History is never alone.
Her secret lover wears the old cologne.
History leaves the door open.

21

The older I get

the more the river means to me.

Time, The Hitchhiker

Time wears a red bandana and yellow flip-flops in the rain.
He talks your ear off while giving you the silent treatment.
Mother wanted a different name, but Father insisted.
Time never listens, he's in a hurry when you are running late.
Grow impatient, and Time takes his sweet time.
Time tags along whether you like it or not.
At stoplights he jumps into the bed of your pickup.
He likes retrievers and whistles at the ladies.
Time loves fast food but shuns the drive-thru.
He makes you pull off at every rest stop but refuses to pee.
Time smokes while you pump the gas.
He never pays but runs up the tab.
Time is the backseat driver who won't show you the map.
Time drinks boxed wine in broad daylight.
He breaks out the weed after midnight.
Time does not believe in deadlines.
He thinks we are all amateurs at keeping time.
Time has no curfew.
He scoffs at time zones but is afraid of Daylight Savings.
Time throws you off track in the final seconds of the match.
After natural disasters Time claims diplomatic immunity.
Time takes The Fifth on a full solar eclipse.
He will set you up, then send you down the river.
Time is a stowaway on a runaway train named Time.
Time likes to watch Spring swing dance with Winter.
He conjures picnic lightning and downpours on clotheslines.
Time flies First Class, hoards the overhead, steals your snack.
Time is the vampire that sucks your time dry.
He is the one-night stand who dines and ditches.
Whatever you do, don't feed Time or his bitches.

Teamwork

Past, Present, and Future on a life raft. No paddle. Past says, last time there was only one survivor. But that was long ago, and he cannot remember. Present insists it is no joke, the wind's picking up. He paddles harder, uses both hands. The others have no hands. The raft spins in circles. Future says, this could be a dark poem, or a parable, which gives Present pause. But Past, ever-hopeful, expects a better future. Present keeps paddling. Meanwhile, just over the horizon, Fate and Luck fight over the helm of a freighter. Truth, in the engine room, tries making repairs, but the blueprints have faded, and the specs are written in a language similar to but different from the six spoken on this ocean.

foghorn –
a woman's form
in the rain

Suddenly

While searching for scissors, I stumble across a note from an old friend I had not heard from in years whose words reappear at the bottom of the junk drawer: *Had we never met I would miss you more...* And this jars loose a quote from a more recent acquaintance: *In addition to extinct, or extinguished, stars, whose wobbly light continues, there are others, much nearer, but so new, we do not yet see them.* On the next clear moonless night, let's haul out the lounge chairs, make camp in the front yard, and stare at a swatch of sky until our eyes glass over. I want to catch a star winking anew, just the two of us making that connection. So many friends in the world we'll never see again. So many more we have yet to meet.

in springtime
everyone secretly
loves you

Sometimes

Sometimes the sky is a balloon
The air heavy. Other times, dry
Wind wicks your eyes.
Sometimes, it is crowded
Everyone elbowing, trying
To make room. Sometimes
We are screaming. Other times
Flying. Sometimes, filling it
With laughter. At rare moments
We hover, speechless, as though God
Speaks to us through the balloon
And all we can do is wave.

Love, A Parable
—for you, Daughters

Once, there were two who met at a park, or party, in the city, or at school.
One caught the eye of the other, just as he or she was parting. Now they
live far apart, on opposite sides of a divide. On one side it is sunny.
A blanket of fog on the other. Neither is a runner, but both get up and go
for a jog. The air, warm or brisk, depending on the side of the divide,
invigorates, and before they know it, they are running, but not at the same
pace. The terrain is difficult, and varied. The light is running out. They run
anyway. They do not know, but they are running toward one another. This
is not a story problem. You will not find it in the logical reasoning sections
of the LSAT or the GRE. At every turn, a fork. Every pass, a new summit
looms. They have so many options, and even more questions. See Dick run.
See Jane run harder. The road's getting steeper. Glazed with ice. The sky is
falling. Always falling. We cannot tell, when we are falling too. It is not
destiny. Not gravity. Not trigonometry. When someone falls for you, he or
she may not have a chute. Only one of you can have it at a time. The chute
keeps swapping, flapping in the wind. The lines tangle; your love needs your
help to figure it out. You reach as you fall. You reach as far as you must.
You reach for all that you can. You grasp the one you trust. Sometimes, you
are facing the right direction.

Yard Watch

You can move cross-country
Settle down, start a family

Call me on Sunday
Or only on my birthday.

I will always be the one
You thought was unafraid

Whose shoulders you climbed
For a better view of the parade.

Even as we breathe apart
We are never close to falling away.

On the coldest days,
You shine in the shadows –

You glow warm
In the blowing rain.

Acknowledgments

Thanks to the editors of the following journals and books in which these poems first appeared in whole or in part.

"Foghorn," *Acorn: Journal of Contemporary Haiku*, San Francisco. 2008.

"Trumpets," *Blue Fifth Review*, 2 June 2017.
bluefifthreview.wordpress.com/2017/06/02/spring-quarterly-spring-2017-17-6/.

"History, the Homemaker." *Crab Creek Review*, Kingston, WA 2017. Fall, 2017.

"Suddenly." *Haibun Today: A Haibun & Tanka Prose Journal*, Sept. 2017, haibuntoday.com/.

"We Fill Our Pockets," Ooligan Press, Portland State University, 2010.

"Sunshine," *Open Spaces Magazine*, Portland. 2007.

"In Springtime," *Orange Linings*, TriMet (public art), Portland, Oregon, 2015.

"Without Supervision." *Plainsongs*, Hastings, NE. Winter, 2018.

"Parhelion," *Suisun Valley Review*, Fairfield, CA. 2017.

"Witnessed on a Country Road," *Tonopah Review*. 2009.
www.tonopahreview.org.

I am indebted to many, including the poets who came before, those in my midst, and the muse who continues to show her face in the faces of my grown daughters. I thank them for letting me be their father, a blessing. I am also grateful to Playa at Summer Lake for a fellowship residency in 2017 where many of the poems in this volume were compiled and edited. Special thanks to Kristin Berger and Judith Montgomery for reading earlier versions, Laura LeHew, Editor and Publisher of Uttered Chaos.

Biography

Scot Siegel is the author of three full-length books of poetry, most recently *The Constellation of Extinct Stars and Other Poems* (2016) and *Thousands Flee California Wildflowers* (2012), from Salmon Poetry of Ireland. He has received awards and commendations from the Oregon Poetry Association, *Nimrod International, Aesthetica* (UK), *Poetry Northwest*, and the Oregon State Library. The late U.S. Poet Laureate, Philip Levine, recognized Siegel's long poem, "Pages Torn From a Schoolmarm's Diary," as a Finalist with Honorable Mention in *Nimrod International's* 2012 Pablo Neruda Poetry Prize Competition. His writing is part of the permanent art installation along Portland, Oregon's Light Rail Transit 'Orange Line'.

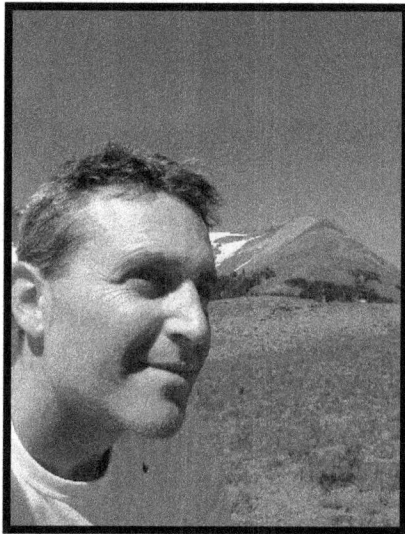

www.ingramcontent.com/pod-product-compliance
Lightning Source LLC
Chambersburg PA
CBHW071243090426
42736CB00014B/3204